KidLit-o was started for one simple reason: our kids. They wanted to find a way to introduce classic literature to their children.

Books in this series take all the classics that they love and make them age appropriate for a younger audience—while still keeping the integrity and style of the original.

We hope you and you children enjoy them. We love feedback, so if you have a question or comment, stop by our website!

Chapter 1: Childhood

Dr. Seuss truly existed. Now, he wasn't a real doctor and his last name wasn't Seuss, but he was a man who left the world a thrilling collection of stories, characters, and drawings that generations of children have loved. Even more importantly, he always remembered his roots, his homeplace, and his values. Here is his story.

In the town of Springfield, Massachusetts, on a road known as Howard Street, lived a couple by the name of Geisel. The husband, Theodor Robert Geisel, was the son of German immigrants who came to America in the nineteenth century. A successful brew master, and he and his father owned a profitable brewery. He married a Miss Henrietta Seuss.

On March 2, 1904, Theodor and Henrietta became parents to a baby boy they decided to name Theodor Seuss Geisel, who they called Ted. This baby boy is the same exact boy who would one day become Dr. Seuss.

Henrietta was a fun-loving, creative mother with an active imagination. Before becoming a wife and a mother, she worked for her father at his bakery. She would invent little chants to remember the pies of the day. When Ted was young and had trouble falling to and staying asleep at night, Henrietta would calm him down with the chants that she created to help sell the pies. From listening to his mother's reciting of those chants at that young age, Ted became familiar with rhythm and rhyming words. Even though he was a little boy, this became a prime influence on him when he became known as "Dr. Seuss."

Mr. Geisel took the trolley to and from work every day. Ted would greet his father each evening once he got home, and Mr. Geisel would hand over the cartoon section of the *Boston American* paper. Ted was captivated by the comic pages.

When his father was named a member of the Springfield Park Board, he sometimes took young Ted along to board meetings. Ted particularly enjoyed accompanying his father to the Springfield Zoo. He would bring along pens and paper and mimic the faces and actions of the animals in his drawings.

During this time, the township of Springfield was flourishing with a number of key manufacturers and a growing population, mainly consisting of German immigrants. The German-American Geisels prospered as well, and their brewery brought them extraordinary success. Young Ted and his sister Marnie were happy children and had a happy home.

Ted spent his free time doing many fun things, as most young boys do, but one of his favorite pastimes was doodling. If anybody opened up his notebooks, they would find the margins littered with drawings and designs of peculiar creatures that were out of the ordinary. Ted also liked to spend time being active in the Boy Scouts. He was a proud member of Springfield's Troop 13. By the time he was a Boy Scout, the First World War had begun.

The World Word I era was not easy for the Geisel family. They suffered much now ridicule because their German background. Ted was teased at school for being a German-American. The local Lutheran church in Springfield even started offering Sunday services in English instead of their usual German-language services out of fear of torment and harassment.

At the same time, Prohibition was a regular topic of conversation in the news, in political discussions, and at the dinner table. The coming of Prohibition would mean money troubles for the Geisels, who kept a roof over their heads from their beer-brewing business. How were they supposed to carry on and pay the bills if people were forbidden to make or drink beer? The brewery was in danger of closing down.

Ted's father did not feel any sense of duty or obligation to Germany; he loved America. The United States was his home. In an effort to display his love for America, he became an active supporter of the Allies, taking advantage of opportunities to express his love for the United States. He encouraged his children to show patriotism. He helped Ted and Marnie have a strong sense of love for and loyalty to the United States.

Patriotically, Ted sold U.S. bonds with his Boy Scout troop. Indeed, he was so driven to sell those bonds that he became the troop's top seller. In fact, he became one of the top sellers in the entire nation. He did so well that he was even scheduled to receive an award from President Theodore Roosevelt, who was president at the time.

At the awards ceremony, Ted took his spot, standing at the end of the line on the stage, eagerly awaiting his award. A bit embarrassed, the president saw that he was short one medal by the time he arrived to Ted's place. President Roosevelt was anticipating only nine boys, since he only had nine medals, and lo and behold, there was Ted, the unexpected tenth boy. The president demanded to know what Ted was doing there. Embarrassed, Ted's scoutmaster led him offstage quickly, but Ted he already feeling humiliated. Not only did Ted not receive a medal on that particular day, but he was mortified by President Roosevelt's reaction to what happened. In fact, this was so traumatic for Ted that he started having stage fright from that point on and dreaded public speaking for the rest of his life.

While Ted might not have been able to get past that particular experience, it did not ruin his feelings towards his birthplace. A common phrase among writers is to "write what you know." Well, Ted knew Springfield remarkably well. Springfield was the kind of place people wanted to call home, the type of town where families wanted to raise their children, the type of town that children come back to in order to raise their own families there. Ted experienced these feelings and had a particularly happy childhood in Springfield.

His imagination often drifted back to this place, his hometown. The town of Springfield had a significant influence on his work as Dr. Seuss. The first book that Ted wrote, *And To Think That I Saw It On Mulberry Street*, is complete with descriptions of Springfield. The red motorcycles that the policemen drive resemble the Indian motorcycles that are famous in Springfield; Mayor Fordis Parker's mirror image shows up. The streams and creeks in Springfield's Forest Park show up in *Horton Hears A Who*. The Knox tractor Ted watched drive on the roads of his town is the vehicle that Sylvester McMonkey McBean drives in *The Sneetches*.

As the First World War came to a close, life in Springfield was good. For the Geisel family, ridicule and threats ended, and prosperity came to the Geisels once again

Chapter 2: Education

As Ted moved became a teenager, he continued to enjoy drawing and making cartoons. He also developed an interest in writing. Ted went to Central High School in Springfield, Illinois, where he wrote for the school paper. He became one of the editors for the *Central Recorder*, writing articles, cartoons, and jokes for the publication.

One of his teachers at Central was Edwin A. Smith, who went by the nickname "Red." Red was a young English teacher who got along well with his students; he was one of the most popular teachers at the school. He had a significant influence on his students. He was a graduate of Dartmouth College, an Ivy League school in New Hampshire. Ted was inspired to follow in his teacher's footsteps.

When Ted turned 18 years old, he graduated from high school and set off for Dartmouth. He had decided to major in English. Ted had a lifelong love of reading and writing; he enjoyed the rhythm of language from his earliest memories of his mother's songs and chants that she share with him when he was a little boy. He even wrote a comedy called *Chicopee Surprised* for his high school in 1921.

Naturally, he was drawn to activities that included writing, and became the editor-in-chief of a humor magazine on campus named *Jack-O-Lantern.* Ted realized through working on the staff that he loved working with words and images.

In addition to the English classes he was required to take as part of his major, he took creative writing courses from W. Benfield Pressey. These would be the only kind of creative writing classes that Ted would ever take. Professor Pressey became Ted's Dartmouth version of Red Smith—he was Ted's favorite professor at the school. The two shared a similar sense of humor. Pressey was a massive encouragement to Ted when it came to writing.

While Ted maintained a strong interest in reading, writing, and art, he was not the strongest student. However, he was always worked hard in the areas he was passionate about; at Dartmouth, this meant *Jack-O-Lantern.*

As the saying goes, all work and no play would make Ted a dull boy. In his final year at Dartmouth, on the night before Easter, Ted decided to throw a party for a few of his friends. Somebody had sneaked in a pint of gin for the friends to share with each other. While parties might have been permitted on campus, alcohol was not. Prohibition laws were in place, alcohol was banned on campus, and drinking was not allowed. The students at the party were clearly drinking at the party, and, unfortunately for Ted and his pals, they all got caught. There were serious consequences for being found with alcohol on campus. All of the students at that party had to go before the dean of the school. They were put on probation for breaking the laws of Prohibition.

The consequences could have been much worse: they could have been suspended, expelled, or even arrested. But for Ted, what was worse than being on probation was his removal from *Jack-O-Lantern.* The college officials fired him from his position as the editor. This didn't keep Ted away from the magazine, though. Nothing was going to keep him from writing. He had to invent a way to continue doing so without getting in even more trouble. After giving it some thought, Ted had the splendid idea to write under a pen name.   He tried a few out, but finally settled on one: instead of writing as Theodor Geisel, he signed his work Seuss, his middle name.

In the spring of 1925, Ted Geisel graduated from Dartmouth College with a Bachelor of Arts degree in Liberal Arts. Ted was going to have to put any dreams he might have had of being a writer or an artist away for a little while. Ted was expected to become a professor one day, not an author; this was his father's dream for him. He applied to Oxford University in England and was accepted into a prestigious program at the university's Lincoln College. Ted planned to move overseas to pursue these studies once he graduated from Dartmouth.

Ted's father was thrilled at the thought of his son studying abroad at one of the best universities in the world. In particular, Mr. Geisel was particularly proud of Ted for receiving a scholarship towards his Oxford education. A proud papa, Mr. Geisel notified the local newspaper, which did not waste any time in printing the good news the following morning. Ashamed, Ted had to tell the truth to his father: he lied about the scholarship. He did apply for the scholarship, but he did not win it. Graciously and generously, Mr. Geisel managed to pull together enough money to fund Ted's schooling in London for the following three years. The autumn of 1925 led Ted to begin his study of literature in the Ph.D. program at Oxford.

Ted studied the epic poem *Paradise Lost* during his time at Oxford. This is one of the longest poems ever written, and tells the story of how Adam and Eve might have come to be in the Garden of Eden. Ted illustrated several large segments of the poem. While the piece contains many vivid images, it is not filled with humor. Ted's take on the poem was original, and he injected his own sense of humor into his illustrations.

He decided to take his cartoons to Blackwell's, a substantial British bookseller. He had hoped that they might want to publish his illustrated version of *Paradise Lost*. Unfortunately, they did not share Ted's funny point of view. In fact, the folks at Blackwells were so angry that Ted would try to make such a serious topic so funny and filled with cartoons that they threw Ted out of the store.

One of the highlights of Ted's time in England was an American girl named Helen Palmer, a graduate of Wellesley College. Although she had secret aspirations to write and edit children's books, she also had an interest in becoming a teacher. The two met in class one day when Helen happened to be glancing over at Ted's notebooks, which were once again filled with drawings and doodles instead of lecture notes. Helen commented on the excellent flying cows that illustrated the lined pages. It appeared to Ted that Helen might have the same zany sense of humor that he had; at the very least, she could appreciate the excellence of his flying cow doodles. The two became friends.

By the end of the course, two things had happened: Ted and Helen fell in love, and Ted had zoned out perfectly on his academics. There weren't any notes on literature anywhere in his notebook; there were only Ted's original drawings.

This was a clear sign that Ted was thoroughly bored by his studies. At the encouragement of a friend, Ted decided to go on a tour of Europe. History books in hand, he spent eight months traveling to all of the famous museums to see all of the places he had studied about.

With Helen's praise and encouragement, it became clear to him that he needed to chase after his dreams and pursue a career as an illustrator. How this was going to happen, Ted had no idea. But at least he felt a true sense of direction about where he wanted life to take him. Needless to say, Ted did not finish his lessons at Oxford.

Chapter 3: Early Career

After Helen finished her English degree at Oxford, she and Ted returned home to America. They were eager to get married and begin a new part of their lives together. However, they were starting out as young graduates without much work experience or income, which prevented them from getting married right away. After all, they needed to be able to afford a place to live and food to eat.

Ted brought Helen back with him to Springfield so they could formulate a plan of what they would do to pursue their chosen professions. Helen was able to find work as an English teacher. While Ted was busy looking for a job, Helen had the idea that he should try to find a job as a cartoonist. She pointed out that Ted had at least three qualities that cartoon artists need to be successful: he was clever, he had a strong sense of clever humor, and he loved to draw.

Ted took a chance and submitted a cartoon to *The Saturday Evening Post*. The sketch features two tourists riding on a camel, exchanging a joke. *The Post* accepted his cartoon, paid him $25, and printed his work in July of 1926. Ted decided to publish his work under the pen name he used during his Dartmouth days: Seuss. However, the *Post* printed his entire name on the border of the cartoon. No matter, Ted was confident that he would be able to build a career for himself at *The Saturday Evening Post.*

Shortly after, Ted used the money he had saved from working on *Jack-O-Lantern* and moved to New York City. He intended to do the same thing at other publications that he was doing at *The Post.* Not every paper was as keen on having his cartoons, though. Luckily, a Dartmouth classmate of Ted's who went by the name of "Beef "Vernon was working for *Judge* magazine. "Beef" introduced Ted to the editor-in-chief of the magazine, Norman Anthony. The editor offered Ted a full-time staff position for a $75 weekly salary.

This was enough of a salary for Ted to feel he could provide for himself and for Helen as a family together. They got married on November 29, 1927 in Westfield, New Jersey. They were finally able to start their life together as a married couple.

Once again, Ted decided to use a pen name on his work. This time, he started signing off on his work as "Dr. Theophrastus Seuss," which eventually came to be just "Dr. Seuss." He was drawing a regular series of cartoons for *Judge* called "Boids and Beasties." These cartoons were filled with the images that are so well known today. Ted decided to add the "Dr." to his pen name to sound more official and more of an expert authority on things.

Trouble started brewing at *Judge*, though. The magazine was not doing as well as it was before. Soon, Ted found his salary cut down to $50 a week. Before long, the magazine decided not to pay their staff in cash anymore. Even though *Judge* didn't have many advertisers, the ones they *did* have paid for their ad space with vouchers. For instance, instead of writing a check to *Judge*, they would provide their services instead. That meant that in order for Ted to receive payments, he would have to use their services.

Helen and Ted wound up spending many nights in Atlantic City, since they didn't actually have to pay for their hotel—it was already paid for, since that is how the hotel had paid for their advertising space in *Judge*. It sounds glamorous, but Helen and Ted would have preferred a normal, paid, cash salary instead.

This time was not always filled with such seeming luxuries: Ted and Helen had made their first home in an apartment in the Hell's Kitchen section of New York City, across from some horse stables. This part of the city was filled with crime during this time period, and living across the street from horses had its own share of problems. Horses would die and be left out on the streets until the Department of Sanitation came to pick them up. All of this was going on, and Ted was still being "paid" with things like hundreds of cases of Barbasol shaving cream, in addition to loads of nail clippers and White Rock soda. The only real perks seemed to be that Ted did not have to worry about writing checks and balancing a checkbook, and at the time, he was not required to pay income taxes.

Needless to say, Helen and Ted worked tremendously hard to move to a nicer apartment in another part of town. Before long other national magazines began publishing his work. His cartoons appeared in periodicals like *LIFE* magazine and *Vanity Fair*. He was able to work as a freelance cartoonist and even branched out into drawing for advertisements. Ted did exactly what he had set out to do: he established himself as a professional cartoonist.

Ted managed to find other work just as *Judge* magazine was entering its final days in the publishing world. One of his recent cartoons depicted a knight fighting a dragon, and the knight was upset that he had just used an entire can of Flit to kill another dragon just a few seconds ago. (Flit was an insecticide, or bug-killing spray, that was sold during this time period.) The Standard Oil Company manufactured Flit, and the wife of one of their account executives thought that Ted's cartoon was quite clever. She was able to convince her husband to hire Ted as a cartoonist for the advertising team.

Ted's ads for Flit bug spray became famous throughout the United States. Every home in America was familiar with the phrase "Quick, Henry, the Flit!" from Ted's cartoons. The Standard Oil Company appreciated Ted's sense of humor and gave Ted creative license with his cartoons. Ted earned a yearly salary of $12,000 from Standard Oil, which gave him and Helen some financial security in the unsteady Depression.

A normal Flit cartoon might have a drawing of huge mosquitoes covering a small child at a family picnic, or some other display of bugs trying to devour people. Someone in the picture would usually have the cartoon bubble near their mouth containing the exclamation "Quick, Henry, the Flit!" It was the first-ever national promotion that came from a funny cartoon. The phrase was the kind of saying that everybody knew, and everyone understood where it came from. It was so famous it became part of radio jokes and comic strips; somebody even wrote a song about it.

Chapter 4: Essomarine

The Standard Oil Company was pretty pleased with Ted's work on the Flit campaign; after all, his ads had brought them steady business and new customers across the country. Money was tight, and Ted was clever and creative, so they presented him with a challenge. They offered him the chance to promote another one of their products called Essomarine, a lubricating oil for boats. The catch was that he had to promote Essomarine with little to no money.

Ted brainstormed with a few other creative colleagues, and the result of their brainstorm was the Seuss Navy. They went to a motorboat show in New York and convinced a few local, wealthy celebrities to pose for pictures in front of gigantic ships, holding up certificates that stated they were members of the Seuss Navy.

These pictures started getting out into the press, which made people want to be in this so-called Seuss Navy. This completely imaginary "navy" became something real: a trendy club that people wanted membership in. The Seuss Navy started hosting large galas with all their members. Ted even wrote an elaborate six-act play for the show one year. He created a character named Essie Neptune. His work drew big crowds, so big that a Seuss Navy Luncheon was held at the famous Waldorf-Astoria Hotel in New York City in 1940.

The press would come and photograph these events. All the while, the reporters would have to mention the product Essomarine. Certainly, Ted met Standard Oil's challenge with great success.

Eventually, the hype surrounding the Seuss Navy died down, as it does with trends. Ted grew bored with his work; after all, the bug spray ads only ran for a few months out of the year and then his work was finished for a while. Standard Oil did allow him to continue his work with publications like *Life Magazine* and *Vanity Fair* since he had a long-term relationship with those magazines.

However, Ted's contract did not permit him to seek out additional work. He was limited in what he could do professionally, yet he still had a yearning in his heart to write. Ted felt that he had finally learned to pair his writing and his artwork together at that through his work Standard Oil. He was often quoted as saying, "It took me almost a quarter of a century to fine the proper way to get my words and pictures married; at Dartmouth I couldn't even get them engaged."

After thinking about it for some time, Ted realized the one area that was not off-limits by his Standard Oil contract was in children's writing. In a later conversation with Edward Connery Lathem, a librarian at Dartmouth, Ted stated the following: "I would like to say that I went into children's book writing because of my great understanding of children, I went in because it wasn't excluded by my Standard Oil Contract."

Viking Press had been paying attention to Ted's cartoons that were showing up everywhere, and the invited him to illustrate a book called *Boners*, which set out to be a collection of children's nursery rhymes and sayings. The book went to print in 1931.   This was the first time that Ted's drawings were in a published book. Unfortunately, it was nowhere near a best-seller and critics thought the writing was boring. (Remember, Ted was not the author of this book; he was only hired to be the illustrator.) On the other hand, Ted's drawings received excellent feedback from reviewers.

This was a defining moment for Ted: perhaps he could pursue his dream of combining his writing and his artwork into a career, after all.

Chapter 5: Beginning of Dr. Seuss

Ted and Helen had not had any children yet, and people kept asking them when they were going to have kids. Ted would usually make the joke, "You have'em, I'll entertain'em." In the meantime, Ted would bring up their imaginary daughter, Chrysanthemum Pearl, when friends would brag about their kids in social conversations. In 1936, the couple was devastated to learn that Helen was unable to have children. (Later on, Ted would dedicate books to Chrysanthemum Pearl.)

Perhaps in an effort to distract themselves, Helen and Ted set off for a trip to Europe, where they had first met. The Geisels sailed on the Kungsholm, a luxury Swedish yacht.

On the way home from Europe, Kungsholm passengers encountered a severe storm that was pounding the ship. They were warned to stay inside due to the gale-force winds. The sounds and rhythms of the boat's engines annoyed Ted. The noises got stuck in his head; he could not get let them go. Ignoring the orders of the ship's staff, Ted visited the lounge on the upper deck. He continued to try to make sense of why he found the boat's current rhythms so catchy and fascinating. Helen, who was a great source of inspiration to Ted, encouraged him to do something creative with this. Thus, Ted sat down at the bar and began to write out some verses.

When Ted finally got off of the ship, he still could not get the rhythm of the rocky ride home out of his mind. He felt crazy. To help himself get rid of the memories of the ship's noises, he continued to add to the verses he had created on the boat. Six months later, Ted paired these lines along with images of his hometown, and thus was born his first children's book: *And To Think That I Saw It On Mulberry Street.*

At this time, Ted was enjoying considerable success as an illustrator: people across the nation were seeing and enjoying his cartoons and drawings in a variety of magazines and advertisements. His clever mind was developing ad campaigns that were memorable. It seemed that if people all over America loved his pictures and his imagination that it would be pretty easy to get a book published, too.

Ted went from publishing house to publishing house with his manuscript in hand. He went to a total of 27 publishing houses in all, and each of the 27 publishing houses said, *sorry, but no, we are not interested…this book is too different…it is too much of a fantasy…there's no market for this book and it won't sell.* Ted kept insisting that these places and images were not altogether imaginary. He argued that the book was based on the real-life events and recollections of life in Springfield. Nonetheless, he wasn't making any progress towards getting the book accepted by a publisher. Sales were everything to them, and making a sale in the Great Depression was harder than ever. If people were going to part with their dollars, they wanted a guaranteed winner of a book. Editors were not so willing to take a chance on Ted; all they saw in him was a risky business move.

Being told no over and over again can wear a person down. Ted felt worn down, all right, and went for a walk throughout the city. He had determined that he would burn the manuscript once he got home to Helen. He had convinced himself to give up on the idea of writing children's books, and that he could be perfectly content creating cartoons for adults, could he not? These were the thoughts going through Ted's mind as was strolling down Madison Avenue in New York City.

Almost out of nowhere, Ted happened to run into an old friend from Dartmouth College named Mike McClintock. Oddly enough, Mike had just started out on his first day on the job with Vanguard Press, a publishing house in New York City. Even more strange and perfect was the fact that he had just started his first day working as an advertising agent in the children's section of the publishing house. Mike volunteered to bring the book down to the office and let his bosses look over it. Within thirty minutes, the Vanguard editors offered Ted a contract. *And To Think That I Saw It On Mulberry Street* had a home at Vanguard Press, who published the book in 1937.

Mike called Ted personally to inform him that the Marshall-Field department store had purchased over 1,000 copies of the book. If Ted wasn't sure if he was an author before, he was unmistakably an author now. Ultimately, the book received excellent views from critics and children's librarians.

This was the beginning of Dr. Seuss.

Chapter 6: The Second World War

Things were going as well as they could be front for Ted and Helen on the home front. The only negative aspect of Ted's journey into writing was the lack of success of his book *The Seven Lady Godivas.* Ted made an attempt to write for adults with this story. Released by Random House in 1939, the cover featured the backside of seven naked ladies, which was appropriate in one way since the story was about these seven Godiva sisters who refused to wear clothing. Only a small portion of the books ever sold; Ted felt like this book was a failure. He returned his focus to writing books for children.

Ted published *Horton Hatches the Egg* in 1940, a book about an elephant named Horton who volunteers to sit on the eggs of a lazy bird friend of his. Ted was continuing to succeed in his pursuit of being an author and an illustrator. However, things in the world at large were not looking as good. World War II was approaching.

If you recall, Ted grew up in a family that valued patriotism and loved the United States. His father and grandfather were active supporters of the U.S. and its role in World War I. Ted supported the stance of the United States during the war. He felt strongly against so-called leaders like Hitler and Mussolini. However, Ted had some particularly strong, negative feelings towards Japan in particular during this war. He made some controversial and rude comments about Japan at this time.

Following in the footsteps of his family, Ted wanted to contribute what he could to the war efforts. He was willing to join the tasks of the armed forces if necessary. Ted began his patriotic work with cartoons. He developed several political cartoons each week for a newspaper in New York called *PM.*

Ted took briefly took some time away from doodling his typical trademark beasties and animals and found himself preoccupied with American war efforts. He once explained, "While Paris was being occupied by the tanks of the Nazis and I was listening on my radio, I found I could no longer keep my mind on drawing pictures of Horton the Elephant. I found myself drawing pictures of Lindbergh the Ostrich." Charles Lindbergh, the famous pilot, was a member of the American First committee, which believed that America should stay out of foreign affairs and wars and should instead concentrate on domestic matters.

Ted became the chief editorial cartoonist for the paper for two straight years, from 1941-1943. During his employment at *PM,* Ted created more than 400 editorial cartoons. This was controversial in some ways since *PM* was known for having a liberal point of view, and Ted tended to share similar politics with *PM.* (He was a registered Democrat.) Ted's work mocked members of the America First committee, known as isolationists. The cartoons made fun of enemy dictators like Mussolini and Hitler. Ted also used his role at *PM* to make a stand against certain prejudices and to offer comments on how the world should operate. Ted's love for America made him feel protective of his country. He encouraged Americans to buy war bonds and put up posters from military recruiters.

In 1942, which was the early part of the war, Ted was 38 years old. He was not eligible to be drafted into war. After his employment with *PM*, Ted worked with the Treasury Department, illustrating posters to encourage Americans to take a stand in the war, but this still did not satisfy the deep need he felt to be involved with the war.

He tried to work with the navy in its intelligence department, but that did not take off. Instead, he volunteered to sign up for the armed forces. In 1943, Ted joined the U.S. Army. He was commissioned as Commander Captain Theodor Geisel of the Animation Department, First Motion Picture Unit. He was based in Hollywood, California.

Ted worked with Frank Capra's Signal Corps to create films used for training U.S. Army soldiers. His job was to help create and make training films for soldiers and draw illustrations for the U.S. public. Ted also developed short movies to boost the morale of the servicemen. He had the opportunity to work with animation directors from Warner Brothers Studios, the people responsible for the likes of Elmer Fudd and Bugs Bunny. It was through his service with the Singal Corps that he met a man named Chuck Jones. Chuck was an animator who worked in television for Warner Brothers. He directed most of the short cartoons that we know today as Looney Tunes and Merry Melodies.

These short films were animated, like cartoons, and Ted was able to introduce a rhyming pattern into some of the scripts that he was in charge of. Chuck and Ted worked closely together, and the two cartoonists hit it off. Together, they invented the character Private Snafu. Private Snafu was the kind of character who constantly makes mistakes and viewers can easily see how Snafu messes up; this character is an example of what not do in the Army. The Private Snafu films were actually cartoons intended for an adult audience.

In 1945, Ted worked on the film "Your Job in Germany," and "Our Job in Japan." Both of these films focused on post-war peace efforts. Two of Ted's films were nominated for Academy Awards: "Hitler Lives" and "Design for Death." He also earned a earned a Legion of Merit award during his time of service

Chapter 7: After World War II

When the war was over, Ted and Helen decided to make their new home on the west coast in La Jolla, California. The Geisels bought an old observation tower to live in, and they referred to their house as The Tower. Ted loved to write in the tower. In 1950, he wrote *If I Ran The Zoo.* While this may not have been one of his most famous books, something famous happened because of it: this is the first book that contains the word *nerd*.

His time in Hollywood allowed him to make some strong connections on the west coast, and Ted wrote the script for "Gerald McBoing-Boing, " which went on to win the Oscar for Best Cartoon Short in 1951. This film was rated #9 of the fifty greatest cartoons in 1994. The National Film Registry chose to preserve this film in 1994. What was so groundbreaking about this animated feature? The little boy who is the star character does not use words to communicate; he only uses noises and sound effects. This idea was unheard of at the time.

However, Ted was not interested in continuing a career in making movies; at the end of the day, he wanted to be a writer and an artist.

Even though World War II was finally over, Ted was still bothered by many aspect of the war, very much the same way he was bothered by the sounds of the Kungsholm storm. Ted traveled to Asia in 1953, making friends with a professor from Kyoto University when he was in Japan. He saw the destruction of the atomic bomb and witnessed how people were living. Ted saw how America was treating the Japanese after the war was over, and he was appalled. He quickly got over his previous negative thoughts towards the Japanese and the bad feelings he had accumulated since the war.

When he got back home to LaJolla, he decided to write a book about his experiences. Ted spent hours each day working on ideas, sketches, and drafts of stories for children. He wanted to write something that would actually show people that it is important for the big guy to stand up for the little guys. These thoughts would become the basis for the story about an elephant known as *Horton Hears A Who!* The book features Horton the Elephant, a character from one of Ted's earlier children's books. Even though Ted usually stayed away from writing stories with an obvious moral, he felt that the lesson behind *Horton Hears A Who!* must be shared. "A person's a person, no matter how small," one of the famous lines from the book, sums up the lesson that Ted was trying to teach his audience.

In 1954, a book and an article came out called *Why Johnny Can't Read*. The authors were angry and frustrated. They believed that many children had no interest in learning how to read or becoming better readers because the first primer books were so dull. The authors believed that the stories and drawings were boring, and there was no way that a child would buy into them.

The two publishing houses—Random House and Houghton Mifflin (Vanguard Press) joined together for a special project. It was unheard of to share a writer, but they managed to work out the contracts—Random House would keep the rights to sell the book in stores, and Houghton Mifflin would keep the rights to make the book a textbook for schools. The publishers wanted Ted to write a book in response to *Why Johnny Can't Read.* Ted's job was to write a new primer for children using only 250 vocabulary words, words that brand-new readers were expected to learn and know. The result of the project was *The Cat in the Hat.*

Ted wrote *The Cat in the Hat* using only 236 words; 220 of these were words geared towards early readers and the remaining 13 were words needed to tied the phrases together. Even though it was a relatively short list of words that needed to be included in the book, it took him nine months to complete. That short list proved to be a challenge, and Ted used his sense of rhyme and rhythm to get around that challenge. He sought out words that rhymed and matched, and invented the story around the idea.

Children loved the book. Parents loved the book. Librarians loved the book, too. Everyone was crazy about *The Cat in the Hat*, but schools were initially afraid to use it in place of their current *Dick and Jane* primers. Eventually they caught on and Ted's book became the standard tool for teaching early readers the basics. In fact, the impact and success of *The Cat in the Hat* was so great that Random House launched a brand new department within their company, called Beginner Books. Based on the ideas in *The Cat in the Hat*, Beginner Books set out to draw children into the world of reading through the use of rich colors, fun images, and imaginative stories.

Released in 1957, *The Cat In The Hat* was Ted's thirteenth children's book, but this was the book that ended up defining his entire career. Within three years, the book sold almost one million editions. Ted didn't lose steam after *The Cat In The Hat*. He wrote *How The Grinch Stole Christmas* in the same year.

The Grinch is perhaps one of Dr. Seuss' best known stories. Ted came up with the idea one morning while he was brushing his teeth. It was the day after Christmas, and he had noticed that he looked super grumpy in the mirror. He barely recognized himself. Ted didn't think that this is how someone should appear right after such a joyful holiday. He wrote *The Grinch* as a sort of way to explore a different part of himself that existed.

The Cat and The Grinch are two entirely different characters, yet Ted always felt like they were the two who were the most like him, personally. Even though he had a license plate on his car that read "GRINCH," the silliness and wackiness of The Cat were such an important part of Ted's personality. In fact, he even wore crazy, silly hats as kinds of "thinking caps" when he was writing. Ted even kept a closet full of hats at the house for distributing to guests at dinner parties.

Following the success of *The Cat In The Hat*, Ted and Helen felt like they could do something more with children's books. After all, *The Cat In The Hat* wiped Dick and Jane out of the water. Along with Phyllis Cerf, they started a division of Random House called Beginner Books. The fall of 1958 saw the launch of this new department, and Ted released *The Cat In The Hat Comes Back* as the first in the Beginner Books series.

While all of these great things were going on in the world of children's literature, Ted still felt that something was missing. He had been affected greatly by World War II and continued to feel passionate about what happened during the war and following it. Ted chose to fuel that that passion into his writing.

Strange as it may seem, it's true; Ted wrote rhyming books for children and beginning readers that seemed innocent on the outside, but the inside of the stories contained a much deeper meaning than the limerick-styled poems that Ted wrote. Ted's personal and political opinions helped him write *Yertle The Turtle* (1958). This children's book was something much more than a normal children's book, kind of like *Horton Hears A Who!*

Yertle The Turtle was written in the style of poetry known as anapestic tetrameter. If you break down the term, you might see the words "an," "pest," and "meter." Think about it as a few pests in a meter; basically, there are two weak syllables followed by a strong beat—the beat "beats" the weak pests away. The rhythm sounds like this: "And today the Great Yertle, that Marvelous he/is King of the Mud. That is all he rhythm can see." Most of Ted's books were written in this style of rhythm. In fact, many of the great British poets used this style of writing in their rhythm, too.

Yertle The Turtle tells the story of Yertle, the ruler of the pond of turtles. Yertle keeps using his turtle subjects to climb up to the top of the pond, rising up on their backs. All of the turtles are in great pain because of Yertle's standing on their shells. Mack, the turtle stuck at the bottom of the pond, is in the most pain. Yertle shows him no kindness as he continues to try to stand above the rest of the turtles and expand his empire. Mack finally decide that he had had enough of Yertle, and lets out a massive burp to knock down the turtle tower that Yertle had assembled and freeing the rest of his turtle friends.

Yertle The Turtle might be a nice story for children, but Ted was using the plot of the story to communicate his views on World War II dictators like Hitler. Along the same lines, Ted penned *The Sneetches* in 1961. This book might seem like a normal children's book with nursery rhymes, but it really is a book about Ted's personal views on anti-Semitism and prejudice: the Sneetches who wear green stars on their tummies think they are better than the other star-less Sneetches, who become the victims of their discrimination.

In between Yertle and The Sneetches, Ted wrote *Green Eggs and Ham*. Much like the challenge set before him with *The Cat In The Hat*, Ted had a limit on vocabulary for this book. Ted accepted a bet from a publisher named Bennett Cerf that there was no way he would be able to write a book using fifty words or less. Cerf believed it was impossible for anybody to create a book based on so few words. He created the story of a boy named Sam-I-Am, who loves green eggs and ham, and tries to get an older, crotchety character to like them, too. The result of this bet was the final copy of *Green Eggs and Ham*, which did contain just fifty words. Those words were: a, am, and, anywhere, are, be, boat, box, car, could, dark, do, eat, eggs, fox, goat, good, green, ham, here, house, I, if, in, let, like, may, me, mouse, not, on, or, rain, Sam, say, see, so, thank, that, the, them, there, they, train, tree, try, will, with, would, you.

Ted not only won $50 from Bennett Cerf, but *Green Eggs and Ham* became his best-selling book ever; it was also the fourth best-selling children's book of all time.

Chapter 8: Later Life and Career

Even though he had successfully published several other books for children, the critical acclaim and rave reviews of *The Cat in the Hat* guaranteed Ted's place as a prime author in the field of children's literature. Many other books came out following *The Cat in the Hat*, and Ted was finally able to live out his dream of being a writer and an illustrator.

The late 1960s brought many changes to Ted's life, one of which was seeing his work come to life. In 1966, Chuck Jones, Ted's old friend from his Army days, rang him up and asked him how would he like to see *The Grinch* animated? As a life-long cartoon artist, Ted could not say no. The two had enjoyed working together on the Private Snafu films back in the day. The men agreed to make a made-for-TV movie of *The Grinch.* The animators used techniques that were being used at Disney studios, which required over 25,000 sketches for the animated feature.

Ted learned about adaptation during this time: how long would the program be? How long should the story be? What parts do we keep, and what can be removed, if anything at all? How do we keep this an entertaining story with a moral value, but not appear too religious? What color should the Grinch be? (Ted was extremely insistent about the colors for *The Grinch*.) Lastly, which actors should they hire to do the voices for the characters? Boris Karloff was chosen to do the voice of the Grinch, even though Ted hesitated about this choice in the beginning. Boris Karloff was famous for being Frankenstein in all of the Frankenstein movies, and Ted was afraid that might be a little too scary for small children. Thurl Arthur Ravenscroft, better known as the voice of Tony the Tiger from the Frosted Flakes commercials, sang the famous song, "You're A Mean One, Mr. Grinch," although Karloff sometimes receives that credit accidentally.

Ted was quite careful not to let the other folks working on this project sway him; The Grinch was his creation, after all. The film premiered for the 1966 Christmas season, and it was the first Dr. Seuss story to make it to film or television.

While this should have been a happy, exciting time in Ted's life, there was something much more painful and drastic going on behind the scenes. Helen had been suffering since 1957 from a disease called Guillain-Barre syndrome, which left her partially paralyzed. Her symptoms were getting worse as the years went on. On top of all of this, Helen had been diagnosed with cancer. She began to suffer from depression because of dealing with these illnesses. To make sad matters even worse, Helen had learned that Ted was having an affair with their longtime friend Audrey Stone while she was going through all of this. Tragically, Helen committed suicide in October, 1967.

Ted was surprised, angry, sad, and depressed—all the things that you would imagine someone would feel going through this experience. For an entire year, Ted did not write.

Ted married Audrey Stone on June 21, 1968. They took a short honeymoon to South Lake Tahoe. The two of them traveled together to exotic places like Africa and threw dinner parties for friends. Their dinner parties were famous, and Ted would often pull out bizarre hats from his hat collection for their guests to wear. Audrey, eighteen years younger than Ted, was a source of fresh ideas and energy to Ted, from suggesting colors to use in his sketches and drawings or the idea for him to grow a beard, which he had never done in his life. Ted felt rejuvenated at a time in his life when he feared growing older and that that things could be slowing down. This inspired him to write several more books, including *The Lorax.*

Similar to his previous books, *The Lorax* discusses more than simple story lines and rhymes. This book is a testament to Ted's view on the environment and nature. Ted decided to use his invented character of the Lorax to "speak on behalf of the trees" and warned against cutting down trees and hurting the Lorax's environment. Long before it was cool to "go green," Ted made his remarks about how humans are destroying the Earth. This was one of Ted's most controversial stories. A group of loggers was so upset by the book that they penned their own version in retaliation called "The Truax." The original *Lorax* contained a line about things being "bad up in Lake Erie," and after improvements were made to Lake Erie, the Ohio Sea Grant Program begged Ted to remove the line from the book. These days, you cannot find mention of Lake Erie in current editions of *The Lorax.*

Ted continued to put out several books a year, such as *The Foot Book, Mr. Brown Can Moon, Can You?* and *I Can Lick 30 Tigers a Day! And Other Stories.* He was constantly finding sources of inspiration, but his drawings maintained the same look and bits and pieces of Springfield always came through in his books.

Now, while his young readers did not really pick up on any political messages in his stories, intelligent adults could see where things were going. In 1974, the political newspaper columnist Art Buchwald challenged Ted to write something that stated his point of view on a political topic, but not in his usual way of doing so.

Never one to back down from a bet or a challenge, Ted took a copy of his book, *Marvin K. Mooney Will You Please Go Now!* and every time Marvin's name was mentioned, Ted crossed it out and wrote in the name *Richard M. Nixon* instead. Marvin K. Mooney was about a little boy whose bedtime has come and gone, and everyone is asking him to go; likewise, Richard M. Nixon was the president at this time, and there were many scandals related to his time in office, and there was a lot of pressure from both the American public and the American government for him to go, too. Art Buchwald printed this version of Ted's story, and within nine days, Nixon resigned from office. Now, it is unlikely that this was the reason the president resigned, but you never know.

In 1984, Ted received the Pulitzer Prize for the entire body of his literary work. The Pulitzer organization selected Ted to receive this prestigious award "for his special contribution over nearly half a century to the education and enjoyment of America's children and their parents."

At this point, Ted had started suffering from one sickness or another before he was ultimately diagnosed with having throat cancer. He spent many hours in doctor's offices, waiting rooms, and hospitals. In his usual Ted way, he grew bored quickly and his still-sharp imagination started wandering again. He started to sketch out the scenes and image s around him. These images results in the hilarious book *You're Only Old Once! A Book For Obsolete Children.* The book came out March of 1986, on Ted's birthday. This was the first book for adults that Ted had written since *The Seven Lady Godivas* in 1939. It made it all the way to the number one spot on the *New York Times* bestseller list and stayed on that list for over a full calendar year.

Chapter 9: Legacy

As the years passed, Ted slowed down his workload. He received some honors and awards in these later years: he received an honorary doctorate degree from his alma mater, Dartmouth College as well as the Laura Ingalls Wilder medal for children's literature in 1980. Ted spent time with Audrey and her two children and took strolls through his garden.

In 1990, Ted published his final book called *Oh! The Places You'll Go.* It is both odd and fitting that this book was the last one of his to be published during his lifetime, since the central theme of the book is about the ups and downs along the journey of life. This book might be the easiest book for readers of all ages and audiences to relate to. Even though it has several characters, a narrator, and a main character, the narrator addresses the main character as "you" throughout the story. This makes it extremely easy for a reader to identify with a main character, since the audience feels like the narrator is addressing them directly.

Ted uses the concept of "The Waiting Place" to warn readers against getting suck in a place where all you do is sit around and wait for something to happen. Ted employs this idea to show that life will happen if you sit around and wait for it to; people need to get out and explore, have adventures and discoveries, and try to enjoy life as thoroughly and as best as possible. This book has become one of the top gifts for people to purchase for high school and college graduations. The National Education Association placed it on their list for "Teachers' Top 100 Books For Children."

Ted was diagnosed with throat cancer and passed away on September 24, 1991. The young boy from Springfield who set out to make a living by drawing and writing had no idea that he would become Dr. Seuss and make such a huge impact on the lives of children everywhere.

By this time, he had published 44 children's books that were translated into 15 languages. More than 200 million copies of his books had been sold worldwide. Eleven made-for-TV specials were filmed based on his stories. Movies have been made based on The Grinch, The Cat In The Hat, The Lorax, and Horton Hears A Who! *Seussical*, a Broadway musical based on Ted's books, debuted on Broadway in 2000. Four television cartoon series have been produced centering on Ted's work; *The Cat In The Hat Knows A Lot About That!* uses the Cat in the Hat to teach two characters named Nick and Sally about animals. The show has been on the air and running on PBS since 2010. Ted received a Pulitzer Prize for his contributions to children's literature in addition to two Oscars, two Emmys, and a Peabody award.

Upon his passing, his wife, Audrey Stone Geisel, took over the Seuss

The University of California at San Diego wanted to honor Ted and Audrey for all of their work with children and building literacy, so they renamed their library the Geisel Library just four years after Ted passed away.

In 1997, with Audrey Geisel's help, The Art of Dr. Seuss project came into being. This enabled Seuss fans around the world to see his work, first-hand, in galleries and museums. Some items are even available for purchase.

Springfield, Massachusetts, Ted's beloved birthplace, wanted to honor Ted in a way that would help others remember him and remember the things he loved and cared about. They opened the Dr. Seuss National Memorial Sculpture Garden in 2002. This is a perfect tribute to man who loved strolling through his own gardens and loved nature. The park has many sculptures of Ted and his Dr. Seuss characters on display.

The annual Theodor Seuss Geisel Award was created by an association of children's librarians in 2004. This award goes out to "the most distinguished American book for beginning readers published in English in the United States in the preceding year." The book must display a sense of creativity, wonderment, and imagination "to engage children in reading."

Then-California governor Arnold Schwarzenegger inducted Ted into the California Hall of Fame on May 28, 2008. Audrey accepted the honor on behalf of Ted. Ted also has a star on the Hollywood Walk of Fame on Hollywood Boulevard (the star says "Dr. Seuss.")

Dartmouth College has never forgotten its beloved son Ted Geisel. In addition to renaming their medical school the Audrey and Theodor Geisel School of Medicine in April, 2012, Dartmouth students returning from overnight trips with the Dartmouth Outing Club eat green eggs and ham for breakfast upon their return in honor of Ted's book, *Green Eggs and Ham.*

Across the United States, elementary school students, teachers, and parents celebrate Read For America Day. It is appropriate that this event takes place on Ted's birthday, March 2. It is customary for people to wear a cat-in-the-hat hat and host readings of Dr. Seuss books.

While Ted did not live to see all of these awards and honors come his way, he would have surely been flattered, but might not have put too much into them. While he was alive, he felt like his greatest contribution to the world was his donation of a Lion Wading Pool at the Wild Animal Park in San Diego, California.

Does that seem strange? You must remember, dear reader, Ted's childhood days in Springfield, of how he loved looking at the animals in the park when his father would bring him along to meetings, of how he doodled imaginary creatures in the corners of his notebook papers. This part of his life always remained a constant source of inspiration to him as childhood usually does. The experiences we have early in our lives stay with us, and influence who we become as adults. In the case of Dr. Seuss, Ted never forgot who he was or where he came from, and through his stories and illustrations, we can never forget him, either.

.

19209126R00050

Made in the USA
San Bernardino, CA
16 February 2015